D1312267

Jane C. Wright
and Chemotherapy

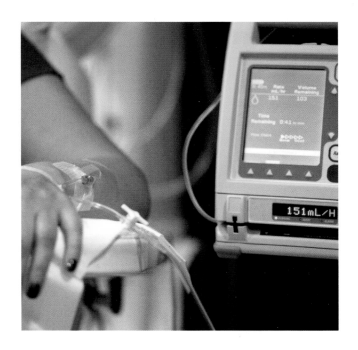

151mL/H

By Virginia Loh-Hagan

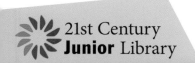
21st Century
Junior Library

CHERRY LAKE
Publishing

Published in the United States of America by
Cherry Lake Publishing
Ann Arbor, Michigan
www.cherrylakepublishing.com

Content Adviser: Kirsten Edwards, MA, Educational Studies
Reading Adviser: Marla Conn, MS, Ed., Literacy specialist, Read-Ability, Inc.

Photo Credits: © Brian A Jackson/Shutterstock.com, Cover, 1; © Monkey Business Images/Shutterstock.com, 4, 12;
© ThePhotosite/Shutterstock.com, 6; © Everett Collection Inc/Alamy Stock Photo, 8; © Rocketclips, Inc./Shutterstock.com, 10;
© Burlingham /Shutterstock.com, 14; © BEKimages/Shutterstock.com, 16; © Peerayut Chan/Shutterstock.com, 18; ©U.S.
National Library of Medicine Digital Collections/Image ID B026209, 20

Library of Congress Cataloging-in-Publication Data

Names: Loh-Hagan, Virginia, author. | Loh-Hagan, Virginia. Women innovators.
Title: Jane C. Wright and chemotherapy / by Virginia Loh-Hagan.
Description: Ann Arbor, MI : Cherry Lake Publishing, [2018] | Series: Women innovators |
    Audience: Grades 4 to 6. | Includes bibliographical references and index.
Identifiers: LCCN 2018003300| ISBN 9781534129108 (hardcover) | ISBN 9781534132306 (pbk.) |
    ISBN 9781534130807 (pdf) | ISBN 9781534134003 (hosted ebook)
Subjects: LCSH: Wright, Jane C., 1919-2013–Juvenile literature. | Oncologists–United States–Biography–
    Juvenile literature. | African American women physicians–Biography–Juvenile literature. |
    Women physicians–United States–Biography–Juvenile literature. | Chemotherapy–History–
    Juvenile literature. | Cancer–Research–History–Juvenile literature.
Classification: LCC RC265.8.W75 L64 2018 | DDC 616.99/4/0092 [B] –dc23
LC record available at https://lccn.loc.gov/2018003300

Cherry Lake Publishing would like to acknowledge the work of The Partnership for 21st Century Skills.
Please visit *www.p21.org* for more information.

Printed in the United States of America
Corporate Graphics

CONTENTS

Doctors can work in hospitals or labs.

A Woman

What happens when you get sick? Most sick people see a doctor. They take medicine and get better. But some people don't get better. They may have a serious sickness, like **cancer**. Cancer is a disease that can cause you to feel sick. It is an **abnormal** growth of **cells**. These cells can invade other areas of the body. Many people have died from cancer.

Although established in 1792, Harvard Medical School didn't admit an African American student until 1850.

Dr. Jane C. Wright was a black doctor. She saved many lives. She's known as the "mother of **chemotherapy**."

Wright was born on November 30, 1919, in New York City. She was born into a family of doctors. Her grandfathers were both doctors. So was her father.

Her father was Dr. Louis Tompkins Wright. He was one of the first black graduates of Harvard University. He was also one of the first black **surgeons**. He created a cancer research center at Harlem Hospital in New York City. Jane followed in her father's footsteps.

Black women doctors had to work harder than others to prove themselves.

She went to New York Medical College. She was a top student. But things weren't easy for her. She succeeded during a time when blacks were not treated fairly. Most doctors were white males.

But she couldn't be stopped. She worked as a doctor for New York public schools. Then she joined her father at his cancer research center.

Ask Questions!

Ask your parents and grandparents about their jobs. What do they do? Do they like their jobs? Are you interested in following in their footsteps? Why or why not?

Only doctors, physician assistants, and nurse practitioners can prescribe drugs.

An Idea

After Wright's father died in 1952, she became the head of the cancer research center. She studied chemotherapy. The **chemicals** in the chemotherapy drugs make it hard for cancer cells to grow and spread.

During this time, chemotherapy was new and untested. Many doctors didn't trust it. But Wright's research changed that.

Some people lose their hair during chemotherapy.
The drug attacks both cancer cells and healthy cells.

Because of her, chemotherapy is now an effective way to treat cancer.

Wright studied how different drugs affected different forms of cancer. She made treatment more accurate. She focused on treating people individually based on their body and type of cancer.

Before Wright, doctors had to remove **tumors** by operating on people. This could be unsafe. Wright figured out a way to use tubes or needles to send drugs to tumors.

She proved that chemotherapy reduced cancer cells. She tested how drugs affected people. She tested to see

Drugs have side effects. They can cause harm
if not used correctly.

if giving drugs in a specific order mattered. She tested to see if **dosages** mattered. She made changes based on how people felt.

This research helped her create guidelines for cancer treatment. She created new ways of giving drugs. Today, more people survive cancer, and it's because of Wright.

Think!

Think of a better way of doing something. Then, test it out. See if it works. How is your way of doing things better? Write down guidelines for others to follow.

Doctors work with governments to create health policies.

A Legacy

Wright saved millions of lives. She made chemotherapy more effective. She gave people hope. Cancer survivors are her **legacy**. She improved how doctors treat patients.

She won many awards for her work. She shared her research. She wrote over 100 papers on cancer research. President Lyndon B. Johnson asked for her advice.

Doctors work with scientists to solve medical problems.

Wright helped create a national network of cancer centers.

Wright worked as a professor at New York Medical College. She became the highest-ranking black woman at an American medical **institution**. She was also the highest-ranking black woman doctor.

Wright worked with other doctors and scientists. She was a member of important groups. She became the New York Cancer Society's first woman president. She formed the American Society of Clinical **Oncology**. Wright paved the way for black women doctors.

Wright helped save lives.

Wright did more than research. She cared for sick people all around the world. She believed that good medical care started with learning about people's needs.

She worked in cancer research for 40 years. She also raised a family. She married a lawyer and had two daughters. She died on February 19, 2013. She loved life and worked hard to save the lives of others.

Create!

Create get well cards for sick patients. Visit a hospital. Give the cards out. Make people feel better.

GLOSSARY

abnormal (ab-NOR-muhl) not normal, in a way that may cause problems

cancer (KAN-ser) a serious disease in which some cells in the body grow faster than normal cells and destroy healthy organs and tissues

cells (SELZ) the smallest units of living matter

chemicals (KEM-ih-kuhlz) substances that are formed when two or more substances act upon one another

chemotherapy (kee-moh-THER-uh-pee) the use of powerful chemicals to kill diseased cells in people with cancer

dosages (DOH-sij-iz) the amounts or frequencies of a medicine or chemical that are used

institution (in-stih-TOO-shuhn) society or organization

legacy (LEG-uh-see) something handed down from one generation to another

oncology (on-KAH-luh-jee) the study and treatment of cancer

surgeons (SUR-juhnz) doctors who perform operations

tumors (TOO-merz) abnormal lumps or masses of cells in the body

FIND OUT MORE

BOOKS

Alagna, Magdalena. *Everything You Need to Know About Chemotherapy*. New York: Rosen Publishing Group, 2001.

Glader, Sue. *Nowhere Hair*. Mill Valley, CA: Thousand Words Press, 2010.

Sullivan, Otha Richard. *African American Women Scientists and Inventors*. San Francisco: Jossey-Bass, 2002.

Watters, Debbie. *Where's Mom's Hair? A Family's Journey Through Cancer*. Toronto: Second Story Press, 2005.

WEBSITES

The ASCO Post
www.ascopost.com/issues/may-15-2014/asco-cofounder-jane-cooke-wright-md-defied-racialgender-barriers-and-helped-usher-in-the-modern-age-of-chemotherapy
Learn more about Wright's career and her involvement with the American Society of Clinical Oncology (ASCO).

Changing the Face of Medicine
https://cfmedicine.nlm.nih.gov/physicians/biography_336.html
Read this summary of Wright's life and achievements.

INDEX

ABOUT THE AUTHOR

Dr. Virginia Loh-Hagan is an author, university professor, former classroom teacher, and curriculum designer. Her first dog died of cancer. She admires all those fighting the war against cancer. She lives in San Diego with her very tall husband and very naughty dogs. To learn more about her, visit www.virginialoh.com.